STEVE MIZERAK'S
WINNING
POOL TIPS

STEVE MIZERAK'S
WINNING
POOL TIPS

STEVE MIZERAK WITH MICHAEL E. PANOZZO

Library of Congress Cataloging-in-Publication Data

Mizerak, Steve, 1944–.

    Steve Mizerak's winning pool tips / Steve Mizerak with Michael E.
Panozzo.
       p.   cm.
   ISBN 0-8092-3428-9
    1. Pool (Game).   I. Panozzo, Michael E.   II. Title.
III. Title: Winning pool tips.
GV891.M688   1995
794.7'3—dc20

                                  95-1637
                                  CIP

Published by VGM Career Horizons
An imprint of NTC/Contemporary Publishing Company
4255 West Touhy Avenue, Lincolnwood (Chicago), Illinois 60646-1975 U.S.A.
Manufactured in the United States of America
International Standard Book Number: 0-8092-3428-9

19   18   17   16   15   14   13   12   11   10   9   8   7   6   5   4

CONTENTS

INTRODUCTION

    Is this a great game, or what? Few sports offer the never-ending challenge and beauty that pocket billiards offers. I know. I've been playing pool since I was four years old. I'm still hooked, I'm still challenged, and I'm still learning.

    I've also picked up a few valuable pointers along the way. The tips contained in this book range from basic fundamentals to advanced principles. They include secrets that propelled my career from being an average player to being a two-time Professional Pool Players Association World Champion and four-time Billiard Congress of America U.S. Open Champion. I hope these tips have the same effect on *your* game!

—Steve Mizerak

CHAPTER ONE

The Basics

TIP 1—STANCE

If you want to be a good pool player, take a stand.

The foundation (both literally and figuratively) of a sound pool game begins with the stance. And the proper stance comes down to a single word: *balance*. Even among the top professionals, stances vary a great deal. The common factor in each case, however, is balance. There *are* some definite no-no's: Your feet should never be too close together, nor spread-eagle. In some ways, your stance at the pool table is not unlike the three-point stance of a football player. Your feet should be a comfortable distance apart, and your bridge hand acts as the third leg of the tripod. With your weight evenly distributed, your balance shouldn't be easily disrupted. Have a friend give you a light nudge from the side and behind. If you're off balance easily, you're not set properly. Your stance shouldn't be too rigid, either. Remember, you have to be able to stroke smoothly and almost effortlessly. Here's another important tip: Use the same stance for every shot. Consistency gives you one less thing to worry about.

TIP 2—STANCE

In pool, you don't necessarily have to keep your chin up.

One of the most often-asked questions I get from beginners is: When I lean over the cue, how close should my chin come to the stick? The truth is that there is no set answer. The distance between your chin and the cue stick is strictly a matter of comfort and sighting. Your head should always be directly over the cue—not to one side or the other. In most cases, the more precise you need to be in hitting the contact point on the object ball, the closer to the shaft your chin should be. The more erect you stand, the less precise your aim will probably be. Some top players tend to stand a little more erect on break shots in 9-ball. They do this for two reasons. First, you don't have to be as precise. You just need to make solid contact with the 1 ball. Second, a slightly more erect stance allows you to generate more cue speed and get more of your body into the shot. A powerful break is absolutely critical in 9-Ball. Experiment with different heights. It won't take you long to determine your best mix of comfort and aiming accuracy.

TIP 3—GRIP

The story behind the proper stroke is a gripping tale.

The key to using the proper grip is simple: relax. The grip is something few players give a second thought to, but I've seen it affect even the top pros in big matches. The tendency, especially on tough shots or in critical points of a match, is to unconsciously squeeze the cue a little tighter. The greater the tension, the more the smoothness and fluidity in your stroke will suffer. Your back hand must remain loose and relaxed. Get into the habit of checking your grip in tough situations. This practice will help you slow down, re-check the basics, and calm yourself before a big shot. All that is really required for a proper grip is your thumb, index, and middle fingers. There should be a little space between the palm of your hand and the cue. Remember, your grip hand is simply guiding the cue in a forward motion. Practice by looking back at your grip hand while stroking. You should notice a little more space open up between your palm and the cue on the backswing. On the follow-through, your palm should come down onto the cue—but don't tighten your grip.

TIP 4—GRIP

Keep your grip out of the pits by embracing the pendulum.

Now that you know *how* to grip your cue, I suppose you'll want to know *where* to grip it. One of the most common flaws I see with beginners and intermediates is that they grip the cue in the same place on every shot. I've also noticed a large number of novice play-ers—particularly men—holding their cue way back on the butt plate. Wrong, wrong, wrong! This may be the easiest and best tip there is: At the point when your cue tip con-tacts the cue ball, your gripping hand should be pointed directly to the floor. Think of your stroking arm as a pendulum. It swings back, then glides forward. Your arm (from the elbow to the wrist) should be perpendicular to the floor at the point of contact. Therefore, if a shot requires you to stretch or use a longer bridge, you'll have to slide your grip hand farther back. On shots in which your bridge hand is close to the cue ball, your hand should be farther up on the cue. In any case, your elbow should be at a 90-degree angle when your tip strikes the cue ball. That allows for maximum accuracy and power.

TIP 5—BRIDGES

As on land, there are tons of bridges in pool. All serve one purpose.

Don't be overwhelmed by the variety of bridges you've seen in instructional books and at the table. Bridges are simply guides to keep the cue stick on its proper course. The key to any bridge is the bridge hand firmly and solidly planted on the table or rail. In most cases, your bridge should allow you to use a level stroke. That's why you don't see players using a high, closed bridge (heel and last three fingers firmly on the table, index finger and thumb encircling the shaft) on the rail. It would force them to shoot down at the ball. Maximum accuracy is achieved when the cue is level with the playing surface. (On rail bridges, the rail itself serves as a nice guide. Just using your index and middle fingers on each side of the shaft will keep the cue in line.) Using an open bridge (either with your hand flat on the table and the cue gliding over the "V" formed by your thumb and knuckle, or by forming a fist on the table and raising your thumb to form a "V") is perfectly acceptable. Most pros use a closed bridge because it provides the most stability and control.

CHAPTER TWO

Ready, Aim . . .

TIP 6—CUEING

Addressing the cue ball requires more than a simple "Hello."

Once you've developed a straight, solid stroke, the single most important element of pocket billiards becomes cue ball control. What happens to the cue ball after you've completed your stroke is at least as important as whether or not the object ball finds its way into a pocket. And the cue ball's path after contact with the object ball is determined by two factors: speed and where your cue tip strikes the cue ball. It's difficult even for accomplished players to strike the cue ball *directly* at its center. That's why it's so important for you to know how the cue ball is affected by an off-center hit. Using a straight-in shot as an example, the cue ball can do only three things: stop, roll forward, or reverse its direction. In pool parlance, those effects are known, respectively, as "stop," "follow," and "draw." The diagram of the cue ball (see page 9) indicates where your cue tip must strike the cue ball for the desired response. (In Chapter 9, in tips about position play, I'll explain the advantages and effects of side spin, or "English.") One of the best tips I can give is that the more often you can execute a shot that hits the cue ball as near to its

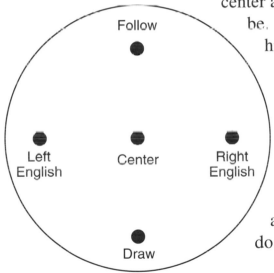

Follow

Left
English

Center

Right
English

Draw

center as possible, the more accurate your shot-making will be. With every degree you deviate from a center-ball hit, your margin of error is increased for several reasons. For starters, the closer you get to the outer edges of the cue ball, the greater the chance of a miscue. Also, when you strike the cue ball to the left or right of center, the ball does not travel straight ahead. Therefore you have to compensate your point of aim. As is the case in most sports, the more things you're forced to take into consideration, the greater your chance for error. Don't try to do more than you're comfortable with.

The key to stop shots is to eliminate spin from the cue ball.

Too many players think that a center-ball hit on the cue ball will make the cue ball stop in its tracks when it contacts the object ball. Not true. First, a true stop shot can only be accomplished on a straight-in shot. I see a lot of players try to stop the cue ball on angled

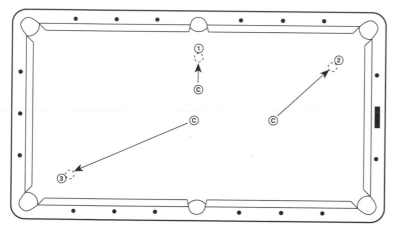

shots. Forget it. It can't be done. Mainly, though, I see players use a center-ball hit on four- and five-foot shots, then look astonished when the cue ball follows the object ball after contact. The trick to the stop shot is that the cue ball must not be spinning when it makes contact with the object ball. When you hit the cue ball dead center, it slides without any spin . . . but only for about a foot. At that point it begins to roll with forward spin—or follow. On shots longer than that, you must strike the cue ball slightly below center. Just as a sliding ball eventually begins to roll forward, so too a ball with draw loses *its* spin after a short distance. The longer the distance between the cue ball and the object ball, the more reverse spin you must apply to achieve a stop shot. The key is to have the reverse spin tucker out at the moment the cue ball hits the object ball. The best way to understand this concept is to shoot the cue ball the length of the table with a center-ball hit. Notice at what distance the ball begins to take on a forward roll. Then, hit the cue ball below center and watch how far it goes before it loses its reverse spin and begins to take on forward revolutions. Also, try the drill depicted on the previous page. Using a moderate stroke, try to get the cue ball to stop on the three shots. Take note of how far below center you had to strike the cue ball to get it to stop on the longer shots.

TIP 8—FOLLOW SHOTS

The cue ball is at your beck and call. Where you go, it will follow.

In the repertoire of pool shots, the easiest to gauge is the follow shot. Yet, it is one of the most useful shots you'll learn. The distance the cue ball follows its contact with the object ball is solely dependent upon the speed of your stroke and how high you strike the

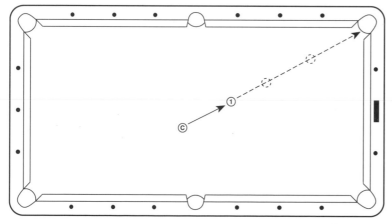

cue ball. The best way to learn and gauge follow shots is to set up a long, straight-in shot. Shoot the same shot several times, striking the cue ball a little higher each time. Note how far the cue ball travels (dotted balls) after making contact with the object ball. Try a firmer stroke. Note how the added speed affects the follow.

TIP 9—AIMING

The easiest way to learn is to start with straight-in shots.

No one can teach you a precise method for aiming. But it is possible to better understand the concept of aim. First and foremost, you should begin taking aim at a shot well before you actually lean over the table to shoot. Begin with a straight-in shot in which your aim is right through the center. The center of your cue tip should hit the center of the cue ball, guiding it through the center of the object ball. While this may seem rudimentary, don't be too proud to practice this shot. Apply the various cueing techniques (center, draw, follow, and left or right English) as you learn them.

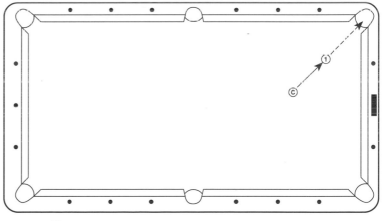

TIP 10—AIMING

The most common mistakes in aiming come on angled shots.

How many times have you used your cue to sight through an object ball on an angled (or "cut") shot and aimed the cue ball perfectly to hit that spot, only to miss the shot badly? Don't be embarrassed. Improper aim on cut shots is the most common mistake an amateur player makes. Why? Because he or she invariably aims the center of the cue ball at the predetermined spot on the object ball. Remember, the contact point is not necessarily where you aim the center of the cue ball. Take Diagram 1, for instance. The broken circle shows where the cue ball would strike an object ball if the shooter

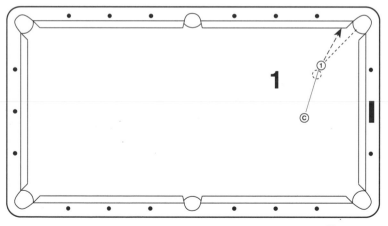

aims the center of the cue ball at the contact point. And you can see where the contact ball ends up. No wonder you always miss that shot! Diagram 2 shows the proper aiming technique. Instead of picking a spot on the object ball, imagine where the cue ball would strike the object ball on a straight-in shot. Then aim the center of the cue ball through the center of the imaginary cue ball. It may seem awkward at first, but once you learn to adjust, the shots will come easily. In Tip 11, I'll show you a drill that will help you get a better handle on aim.

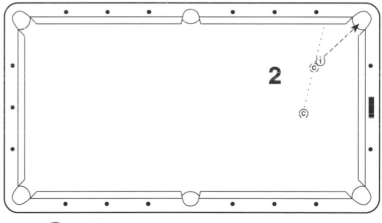

TIP 11—AIMING

Developing good aiming habits is as easy as 1, 2, 3, 4, 5 . . .

Learning to properly line up a shot takes some getting used to. As is the case with many techniques in pocket billiards, repetition is the best teacher. This drill will help you get acclimated to your line of aim. Remember, you should begin aiming *before* you lean over

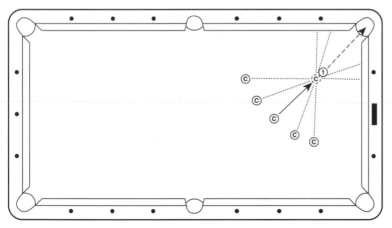

the shot. It's easier to view the placement of that imaginary cue ball while you're standing erect. Start with a straight-in shot, then add a few degrees of angle for the next shot. The position of your imaginary cue ball never changes, but the line through the center of the cue ball (dotted line) changes with the different angles.

TIP 12—AIMING

Being able to shoot along the rail is a slice of happiness.

The shot that seems to draw the widest variety of theories is the one where you must aim at a ball that is frozen to the rail. Do you hit the rail first? The ball first? The rail and the ball simultaneously? The answer is yes. Different scenarios along the rail require differ-ent approaches. The shot shown here is relatively easy. The object ball is resting along the rail, so just use the same approach you would if it was away from the rail. Simply aim as if it were any other shot. Don't try to compensate with English or draw or rail-first contact. And there is no need to hit this shot too hard.

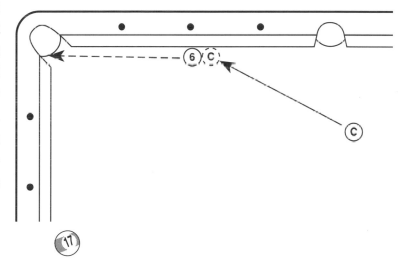

TIP 13—AIMING

Slicing a ball the length of the table demands a different spin.

Longer cut shots of object balls that are frozen to a rail are very difficult, but look great when the object ball hugs that rail for five or six feet. The trick is to hit the rail first, again not using any English on the cue ball. You must strike this shot a little harder be-

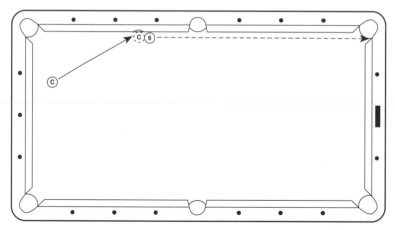

cause you're barely making contact with the object ball, yet it must travel the length of the table. When the cue ball pushes into the rail, it will nudge the object ball slightly off the rail. This is important because I've had my share of long slice shots catch the tip of the side pocket, knocking the object ball off its line to the corner pocket.

TIP 14—AIMING

Steep-angled frozen cut shots require a little English.

The third type of frozen cut shot is the type that occurs when the cue ball is at an angle steeper than 45 degrees. Some players fire the cue ball into the rail, aiming to catch just a sliver of the object ball. Another option is to shoot into the rail first, using left English on the cue ball. (Left English would be spin in the direction of the object ball. If you were hitting to the left of the object ball, you'd use right English.) This approach has the same effect as if you were shooting from the other side of the rail. In this case, don't shoot too hard. You have to let the English do its job.

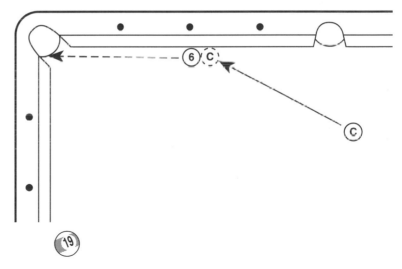

TIP 15—AIMING

It doesn't do much good to rail against long shots.

This is another shot that scares players to death. It looks like it should be easy, but it's actually a shot that takes a lot of practice to master. First, it takes a firm stroke. Not too hard! Some players slam this shot and hope that, even if it doesn't go in, it'll look good!

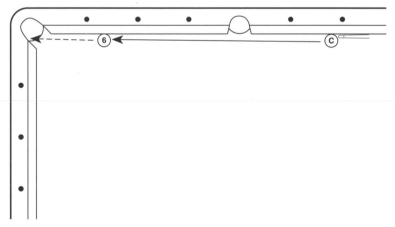

By the same token, you can't baby this shot. Hit it too soft, and the cue ball may wander off its course. The key to this shot is to use inside English—meaning English on the side of the cue ball that is against the rail. That will cause the cue ball to leave the rail slightly, thus avoiding the tips of the side pocket.

CHAPTER THREE

English

TIP 16—ENGLISH

English is as easy as driving on the wrong side of the road.

The trick to understanding English is to think in terms of opposites. If you strike the cue ball on the extreme right side, it will first glance to the left, then, upon striking a rail, will rebound out to the right. The best way to learn English is to use only the cue ball

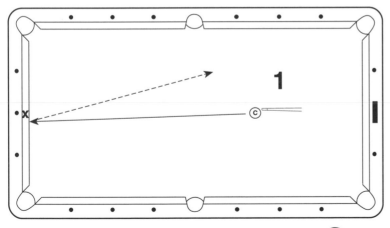

(Diagram 1). Make a chalk mark on the end rail (X). Now, aiming for that mark, strike the cue ball using extreme right English. You'll notice that the cue ball will actually strike the rail to the left of the mark. (A round ball struck near its outer edge isn't going to go straight ahead.) Also, the right spin will cause the cue ball to rebound to the right at a much wider angle. The lesson here is twofold. First, you now know how to widen the angle at which the cue ball exits contact with a cushion. Second, you now realize that, when using English, you must compensate by slightly adjusting your aim. If

that mark was an object ball, you would have missed your shot. Practice the same shot (Diagram 2), only this time adjusting your aim (dotted line) so that the cue ball does hit the mark. It will seem awkward at first, but as you become more proficient, the addition of English to your game will be an enormous help.

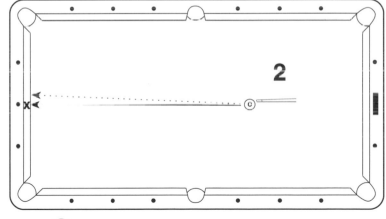

TIP 17—ENGLISH

Hitting a shot two different ways puts a new spin on your game.

It's one thing to sit and explain the different effects English has on the cue ball, and another thing to go out and apply that knowledge. A great way to learn is to set up a shot, striking the cue ball with different spin to gauge the varying effects. The shot in this dia-

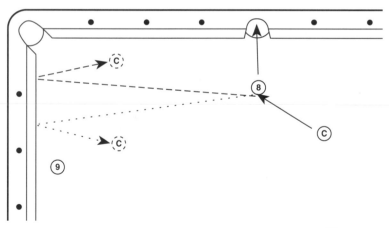

gram shows not only the effect of English after the cue ball hits the cushion, but the effect of English on the cue ball's direction after it strikes the object ball. The dashed line shows the path the cue ball will take when struck with right English. The dotted line shows its path using left English. Which puts you in a better position for the 9?

TIP 18—ENGLISH

Like a second language, English puts a different spin on things.

Players generally apply English to the cue ball because they want the cue ball to react a certain way when it contacts a cushion. But few people take the time to look at English's effect on the object ball. When you put right English on the cue ball, it spins counter-clockwise. When that cue ball strikes the object ball, it transfers opposite spin to that ball, meaning the object ball is now spinning clockwise. This is important, because the spin that's transferred causes the object ball to react differently—namely, it "throws" (dotted line) the object ball off of its natural line (dashed line).

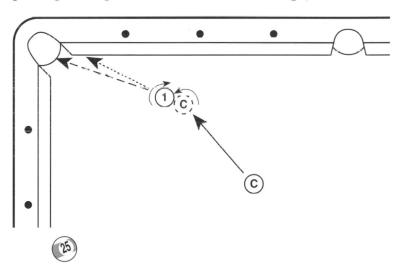

25

CHAPTER FOUR

Angles

TIP 19—ANGLES

Pool is the place to be when it's 90 degrees.

One of the most common problems beginners have is in knowing where the cue ball is going after it strikes an object ball. The easiest way to approach this question is with the 90-degree theory, which states simply that when the cue ball strikes an object ball from an angle, the cue ball will depart along the line that bisects the two balls at the point of contact. That may sound complicated, but it's really very easy. The diagram shows where the cue ball will strike the object ball. The 90-degree line that bisects those balls (dotted line) will be the cue ball's path after contact.

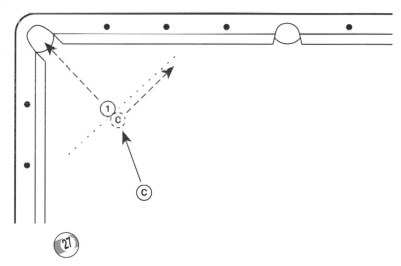

TIP 20—ANGLES

Beat the heat of the 90-degree rule by drawing strength.

Here's another valuable tip: you can cheat the 90-degree angle of departure theory (dotted line) by using reverse spin, or draw, on the cue ball. The draw on the cue ball, achieved by striking it below center, shortens the departure angle from the object ball, even on angled shots. Is this important? It's invaluable. Now you can apply this technique to avoid a scratch, avoid object balls or, as is the case in this diagram, purposely bump object balls to break up a cluster. You'll be amazed at how often a little trick like this means the difference between giving up the table or continuing.

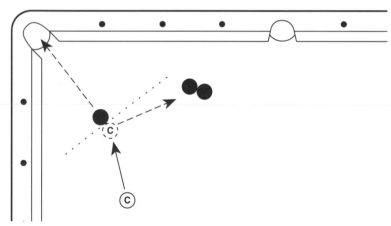

If 90 degrees is too hot, follow a different path.

You can also tinker with the departure angle of the cue ball off an object ball by using follow. Because follow means you've forced the cue ball to roll with forward spin, achieved by striking it above center, it will continue to roll forward slightly even on angled shots. The shot in the diagram shows the natural, 90-degree angle at which the cue ball should depart its contact with the object ball (dotted line). But by using follow on this shot, the cue ball will follow the path of the dashed line. That's important, because the cue ball will now avoid the striped ball for position on the next solid.

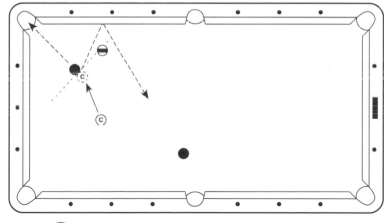

CHAPTER FIVE

Technique

TIP 22—TECHNIQUE

Stay the course with your follow-through.

There are several elements of the stroke I've already discussed. Another important element is the follow-through. Whether you're using follow or draw, the cue tip should always follow well through the shot. Additionally, the tip should never raise up during the follow-through. In fact, a little hint on practicing the follow-through is to exaggerate your stroke a bit and follow through until your tip rubs down onto the cloth. The optimal follow-through is about eight inches. Also, always be sure to follow *straight* through. Don't let the tip deviate at all to the right or to the left.

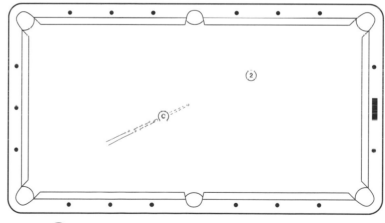

TIP 23—TECHNIQUE

You don't even need a pool table to perfect a straight stroke.

You know the look of astonishment that comes over your face when you lean over a shot, aim perfectly, and promptly miss the shot badly? Nine times out of ten, the problem can be traced to your stroke. You think you stroked perfectly straight, but in reality you probably didn't. What caused your stroke to go off line in such a short distance? Contributing factors include: lifting your body from the shot too soon, gripping the cue too tightly on your final stroke, and simply allowing your stroking arm to waver. There are a few terrific ways to work on your stroke, and, in some cases, you don't even need a pool table! First, when you're at the table, make a bridge along the rail and practice your stroke. Is it staying perfectly parallel with the rail? Another old method, which you can practice on your kitchen table at home, is to lay a Coke bottle on the table facing your cue and stroke the tip directly into the bottle. Place the soda bottle six or so inches away, so that your follow-through is bringing the cue tip into the bottle. (Follow-through is *so* important!) Also, peek back at your arm and elbow to make sure everything is in sync.

TIP 24—TECHNIQUE

The positioning of your bridge hand affects accuracy.

One of the best tips I can offer concerns placement of your bridge hand. It's one of those things that players tend to forget about every so often. There are two simple things to remember when planting your bridge hand onto the table: too close cramps your style and too far lessens your accuracy. Here's why: When your bridge hand is too close to the object ball, you don't give yourself enough room to stroke properly. When your hand is too far away, the cue tip has to reach too far for the cue ball—which makes pinpoint accuracy more difficult. The proper distance is about eight inches.

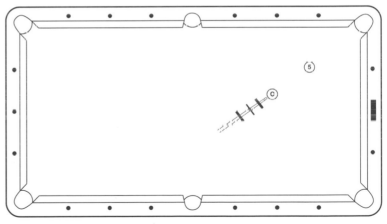

TIP 25—TECHNIQUE

Added speed will result in a radical departure from the norm.

There are certain principles that I try to get aspiring players to remember. But, in some cases, there are exceptions. Take the 90-degree angle of departure theory. In most cases, that theory holds true. We've already seen, however, how to cheat the rule using reverse

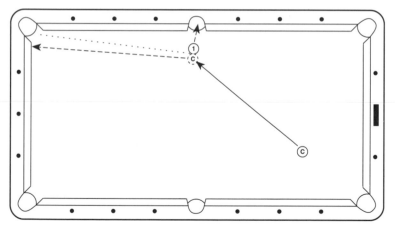

spin. There are times when you'll want the cue ball to depart at a slightly wider angle. Can you cheat the rule again? Yes. The shot in the diagram shows a certain scratch—if you follow the 90-degree rule. But by hitting the ball harder, the cue ball will leave the object ball at a wider angle, avoiding that scratch.

CHAPTER SIX

Practice Drills

TIP 26—PRACTICE DRILL

Circle your wagons, draw your guns, and follow this tip.

No book of instructional tips would be complete without a few practice drills. (Pocket billiard teachers are no different than schoolteachers. Assigning homework and drills is a teacher's birthright!) It's one thing to practice stop shots, follow, and draw on particular

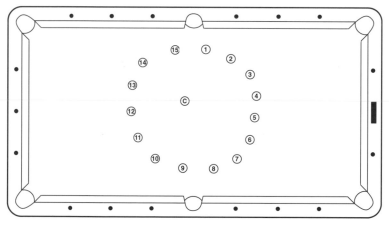

shots, but the best way to learn these techniques is to apply them in a practical manner. In this drill, set all 15 balls in a circle. Start with the cue ball in the middle and try to run all the balls without allowing the cue ball to touch a rail. Using just stop, follow, and draw, you should be able to run out. Shot selection is very important here.

TIP 27—PRACTICE DRILL

One "L" of a way of developing a delicate touch.

The best way to maintain your enthusiasm for any sport or hobby is to challenge yourself. Pool is no different. Don't just throw balls on the table and shoot. Have a plan. Set up a challenge. I always found that if I set up challenging drills, my concentration and determination were much sharper.

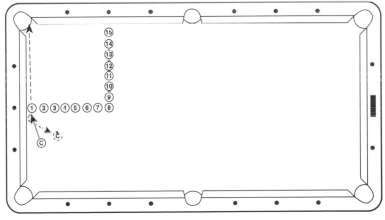

The drill here is called the "L" drill, for obvious reasons. Set up the balls as shown and run them in order. Beginners almost always fail by hitting the cue ball too hard and being out of position for the next ball. This drill is great for developing a soft touch. No cheating! If you miss a shot, start over.

TIP 28—PRACTICE DRILL

The long road ahead is toughest on beginners.

It's no surprise that the toughest shots for beginners are the ones that involve a lot of real estate. Long shots are difficult because your aim has to be extremely accurate. The farther the object ball must travel, the farther off track it will eventually drift. There really

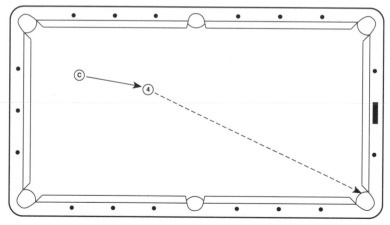

isn't a secret to accomplishing long shots more consistently. Accuracy comes with practice . . . and lots of it. Shoot the shot diagrammed here over and over. Chances are, if you miss, it will consistently either be to the left or right. Make the proper adjustment and keep shooting. Your confidence will soar over time.

CHAPTER SEVEN

Specialty Shots

TIP 29—THROW

If you can't shoot a ball in, throw it in!

When you're just learning the principles of advanced pocket billiards, a lot of the shots and ideas may seem impractical. The value of these principles comes when you can mix two or three together to help bail you out of a tough spot. Here's a nifty little manuever

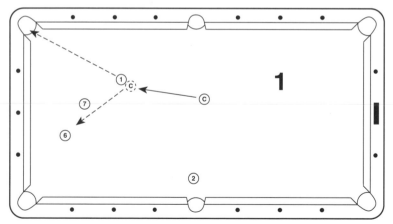

that combines the elements of position play and "throw." The shot (in Diagram 1) is easy enough to cut in, but to get position on the 2 ball, you'll want to avoid running into the 6 and 7 balls. If you could hit the 1 ball almost straight on, you could hold position for the 2. Well, with throw you can. Remember, throw occurs when you apply spin to the cue ball, which, in turn, transfers opposite spin to the object ball upon contact. This "throws" the object ball slightly off its natural line. Diagram 2 demonstrates using throw combined with hitting the object ball almost full (without any angle), which keeps the cue ball from traveling very far and allows you to get the desired position on your next shot. Apply right English to the cue ball, aiming to strike the object ball along the dotted line. When the cue ball impacts the 1 ball, it will throw the 1 slightly to the right and into the corner pocket. The cue ball will stay put, for position on the 2 ball.

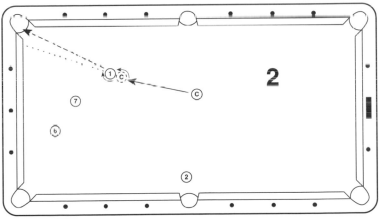

Throw a little twist into your frozen combinations.

One of the more common occurrences, especially in 8-Ball, is when two object balls are frozen (touching at one point). In some cases, the frozen balls are in a direct line to a pocket, making them "dead." A dead shot means that no matter where you contact the first ball, the second ball will go straight into the pocket. Frozen combinations that are not quite dead can still be made by throwing the shot. By striking the 1 ball on the left, the cue ball will actually give the 1 left English. That, in turn, will transfer right English to the 2 ball and will throw the 2 ball into the corner pocket.

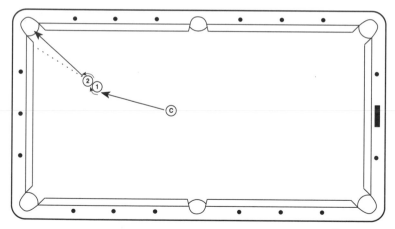

TIP 31—CAROMS

Bumping balls into pockets doesn't have to be an accident.

Every so often when you hit a shot, the cue ball rolls away from the object ball and bumps another object ball into a pocket. Wouldn't that come in handy when an obstructed object ball is sitting in the jaws of a pocket? No problem. By knowing the angle at which the cue ball comes off the object ball (dotted line), it can be done. It comes in handy in 9-Ball. In this case, the 4 ball can't be pocketed. By bumping (or "caroming") the cue ball off the 4 and toward the 9 ball, you accomplish two things: You can sink the 9 and win; and even if you miss the shot, the 4 will be hidden from your op-

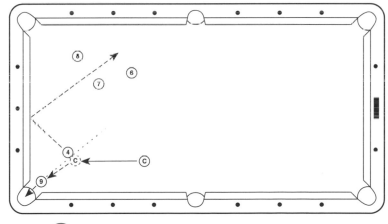

TIP 32—KICK SHOTS

When the tables are turned, go down kicking.

There's little doubt that studying the tips and lessons in this book will help improve your game. As you begin to compete at a higher level, however, you'll quickly learn that you're not the only person who plays pool well! Therefore, you can expect to find your-

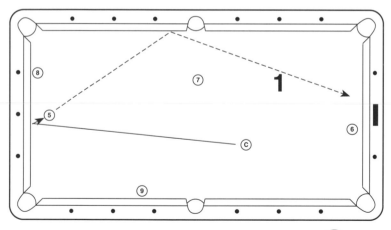

self on the wrong end of a pretty good safety shot every now and again—especially playing 9-Ball. The problem I've noticed with beginner and even intermediate players is that they simply kick at the object ball and hope for the best. Like every other facet of pool, taking the time to develop a well-thought-out plan can pay huge div-

44

idends. The diagrams show situations in which you've been left safe. With some planning, you can return the favor. In Diagram 1, kicking in behind the 5 ball (hitting it as full as possible) will send the 5 to the side rail and up, while leaving the cue ball near the end rail. Diagram 2 shows a ball in the middle of the table. Don't try to kick it into the side pocket. Instead of trying to hit the 5 full, aim to hit the near one-half, sending the 5 to one end of the table, and the cue ball to the other. In both cases, speed is key. Don't try to blast the balls around the table. Maintain control and accuracy.

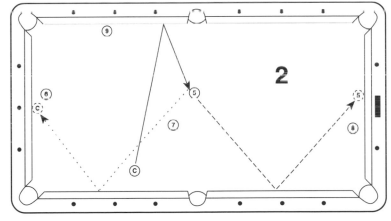

TIP 33—KICK SHOTS

The "bigger" the ball, the easier it is to hit.

Here's a tip picked up from our 3-Cushion billiards brethren. In 3-Cushion, or carom billiards, they commonly use the term "big" ball. No, the ball is no different in size than the others. A ball is considered "big" when it is near a rail, because the cushion offers a

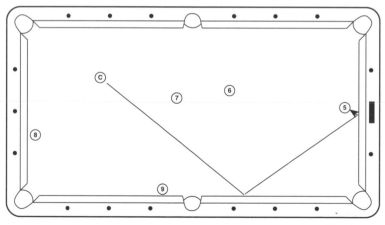

larger margin for error. This comes in handy when you're forced to kick at a ball. If the cue ball is coming in from an angle, you always want to aim for the back side of the object ball. You don't have to be as precise, because the cushion is there to help if your aim is slightly off. If the rail offers its assistance, take it!

TIP 34—KICK SHOTS

Sometimes the only way to bank a ball is to sneak up on it.

This is, at best, a high-risk shot. But sometimes it's your only shot. The game is 8-Ball, and you're down to your last ball. A safety isn't really available. A conventional bank shot has some obvious pitfalls—the balls are too close and a double-kiss (in which the object ball would bump back into the cue ball after hitting the rail) looks pretty inevitable. Your only option is to kick in behind your ball, rail-first. There is no surefire way to aim this shot, but what you try to do is visualize where the cue ball would be if it was a straight-in shot (dotted cue ball).

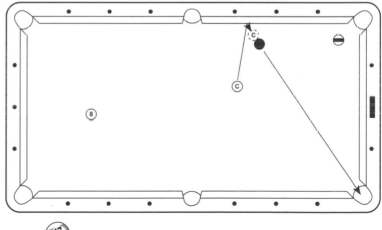

TIP 35—BANK SHOTS

A few simple rules will accommodate all your banking needs.

The best advice on banking that I can give is to avoid all of the tricky geometric formulas and stick to a couple of basic, sound principles. First, do not attempt bank shots that require you to cut the object ball in an attempt to create the proper rebound angle. Those are stabs in the dark. Stick with shots in which you shoot straight on and the "natural" angle brings the object ball to or near the intended pocket. The diagram shows just such a shot. Shooting straight on, the object ball's angle approaching the rail is roughly the same as its angle leaving the rail. Another tip: Don't try to kill the ball.

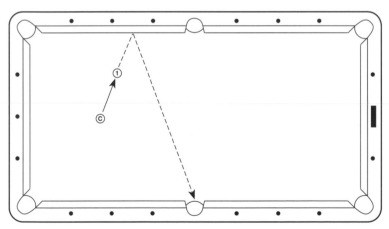

TIP 36—BANK SHOTS

For the best rate of return, banks prefer corner locations.

A big misconception out there is that side pockets have larger openings than the corners. It's an optical illusion. Corner pockets are always your best bet, especially on bank shots. The diagram shows the cue ball in perfect position for banking a striped ball cross-side or a solid ball cross-corner. For the money, which would you choose? I know I'd choose the cross-corner. The side may look more inviting, but the corner is far more forgiving. As the solid rolls toward the corner it can glance the bottom rail and/or the outside pocket edge and still go in. The cross-side has to be dead center.

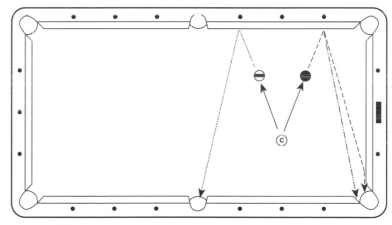

TIP 37—BANKING

There *are* ways to shorten and lengthen angles on banks.

Don't be upset if you view the natural angle of a bank shot and find that it's probably going to miss the pocket by an inch or two. Let me show you the easiest way to shorten or lengthen the departure angle of an object ball off the rail. Simply adjust the power of your stroke! If the natural angle of a shot looks like the object ball will come in short of the pocket (see solid line in diagram), you can compensate by striking the cue ball softer than normal (resulting in the broken line path). Conversely, if the natural angle is going to send the object ball long, a firmer stroke will shorten the angle.

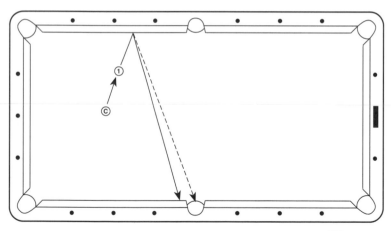

TIP 38—BANK SHOTS

Unless you know the trick, frozen banks can be slippery.

The basic premise of bank shots is pretty simple. But what happens when the ball you want to bank is frozen to a rail? Frozen banks are much more difficult than normal banks. First, it's harder to judge the exit angle from the rail. Also, there is the hazard of the double-kiss—which happens if the cue ball isn't out of the way when the object ball begins its movement away from the rail. The key is to strike one side of the object ball (see diagram), and use reverse spin to draw the cue ball away as quickly as possible. You must hit this shot hard. Soft shots increase the likelihood of a double-kiss.

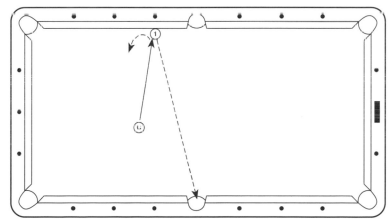

TIP 39—KISS SHOTS

If you know what to look for, kiss shots are easy!

There are several types of kiss shots in pocket billiards. One type occurs when two object balls are touching, or frozen. Too often, players fail to stop and give the frozen balls closer inspection. In some cases, the balls are linked in such a way as to make one of

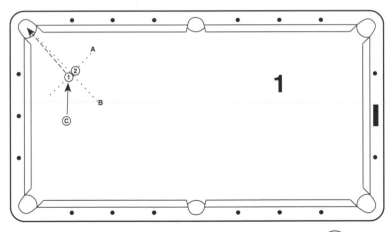

them perfectly dead—meaning that, upon contact, one ball will help guide the other directly into a pocket. On these dead shots, it's practically impossible to miss. Spotting a dead shot is relatively easy. Simply visualize one line through the center of the object balls (dotted line A) and another between the balls (dotted line B). If line B cuts directly through line A and into a pocket, the shot is dead. In Diagram 1, as long as the cue ball strikes the 1 ball somewhere between those crossing dotted lines, the 1 ball will scoot obediently into the pocket. If the cue ball is on the other side of that intersecting line (see Diagram 2), then the 2 ball is the ball that is dead to the corner pocket. Don't be intimidated. This is a valuable tip to know, and it's not nearly as complex as it sounds. And, like I said, once you learn to recognize dead kisses, you'll love them because they're almost impossible to miss!

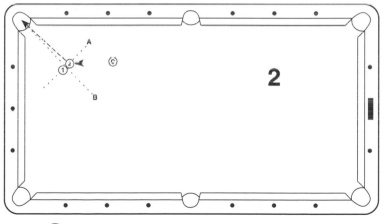

TIP 40—RAIL-FIRST SHOTS

Don't let a little thing like an obstructing ball stop you.

Many beginners get frustrated when they step up to the table with no clear shot to take. But just because there is no clear, direct path to a "pocketable" object ball doesn't necessarily mean that you can't pocket that ball. In this diagram, the path to the 1 ball is ob-

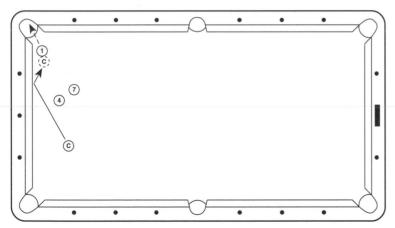

structed by several object balls. The key thing to remember here is that to pocket the 1 ball, the cue ball must contact it as shown by the broken circle. How you get the cue ball to that spot depends a lot on your imagination. Don't forget the option of going rail-first. On a shot like this, the rail-first option is easy and safe.

TIP 41—KICK SHOTS

Every once in a while, a swift kick will get you back on track.

How many times have you come to the table with an object ball dangling at the edge of a pocket, and you can't get at it? It seems to happen a lot. That's where knowledge in kicking becomes helpful. One way to look at kick shots is to think of them as bank shots

without an object ball. The shot diagrammed here shows a layout in which there is no direct shot at the 5 ball. Don't fret. Treat the shot like a bank shot and simply send the cue ball cross-corner. This is somewhat similar to a rail-first shot (shown in Tip 40), only the distance into and out from the rail is longer.

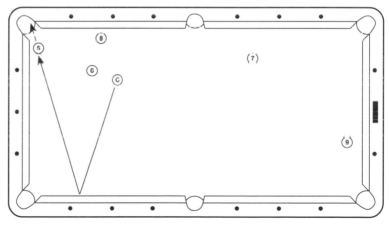

TIP 42—DEAD BALLS

Look closely. You may just find a diamond in the rough.

You've received advice on shooting at the ball closest to the pocket and advice on dead combinations. So which would you choose if both came up in an 8-Ball game? The diagram shows two balls (a and b) relatively close to pockets. Which would you shoot?

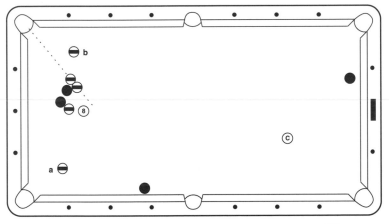

Well, actually, if you look closer, you'll see that the two corner balls in the cluster are dead (dotted line) to the corner pocket. Since dead balls are almost impossible to miss, they are your best bet. Just another example of checking all options before shooting.

CHAPTER EIGHT

Shot Selection

Direct deposits are always preferred to high-risk banking.

While it is worthwhile to learn proper banking principles, always keep in mind that directly pocketing object balls is the preferred route to take. Too often players eschew what looks like a difficult cut shot in favor of what appears to be a simple bank shot. Looks

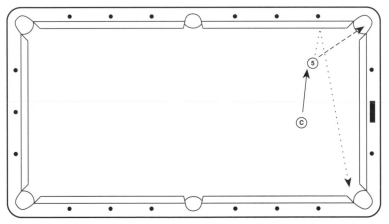

can be deceiving. Here, the cut shot (dashed line) is pretty thin and the bank (dotted line) looks relatively safe. Still, the cut shot is the better alternative because your aim is the only variable. When you bank the ball, you're adding variables—primarily the unknown response of the cushion. Will the ball rebound at a true angle? Go direct.

TIP 44—SHOT SELECTION

Do you recognize trouble when you see it? You'd better!

No matter what pocket billiard discipline you're playing, you must be able to recognize trouble spots before it's too late. Learn to give the table a good look before you begin pocketing those easy shots. The reason? If there are three or four balls tied up in the same

general area, you're going to have to break them apart sooner or later. To do so, you often must use a shot that will allow you access to that cluster (as shown in the diagram), or you must know how to play a safety shot that will force your opponent to address the issue. Either way, early recognition of the situation is the key to success.

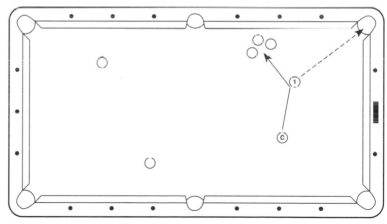

Don't make things tough on yourself at the very start.

All too often, I see players begin a rack by choosing a risky, difficult shot. They may think that making the shot will open the door to an easy rack, but in reality they are risking a total sell-out. Remember, when you miss, your opponent gains control of the table.

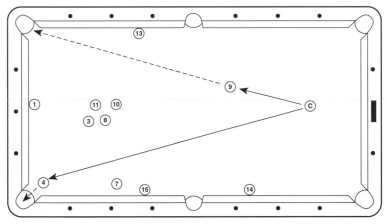

That may sound simple, but control of the table is the key to success. At the start, look for the easiest shot on the table, and go from there. In the diagram, the 9 ball may look easy, but there is too much distance between the 9 and the corner pocket. Here, select the 4 ball. It's safer and will help you maintain control of the game.

CHAPTER NINE

Position Play

TIP 46—POSITION PLAY

The game's real challenge comes from position play.

So much focus, especially for beginners, is placed on pocketing a single ball. That's all fine and good, but the challenge and ultimate enjoyment from the game comes when you can manuever around the table to run a number of balls in succession. The concept is ob-

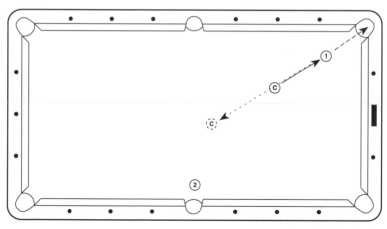

vious: Approaching a shot, you must determine how to get the cue ball in position to make the next shot. Virtually all shots offer several options. Some don't. Here, because the 1 ball is straight in, your only path for position on the 2 ball is reverse, or draw. The tendency on draw shots is to over-stroke. Keep your stroke smooth and easy.

TIP 47—POSITION PLAY

Learn by playing a two-ball game.

Learning to play position can be frustrating. You look the table over and plot your course. But then, if you get even a little out of line, your whole plan is ruined! It always helps to break things down to their simplest form. Try this exercise. Throw two balls out on the table. Pretend they're the last two balls in the game—it could be the 8 and 9, or the last solid and the 8 ball. Now, with cue ball in hand, finish the game. One of the keys is to play for a general area, not an exact spot. It's not as easy as it looks, but it's a great way to get your mind working. And remember, play for a zone, not a spot.

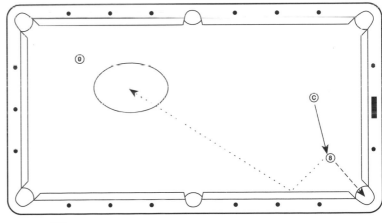

When playing for position, toe the line. Don't cross it.

Here's some great advice for position play: When you're determining position on your next shot, don't try to be too precise. I see it happen all the time. Players leave themselves one tiny little area for the cue ball. Trying to be too fine is extremely tough. You

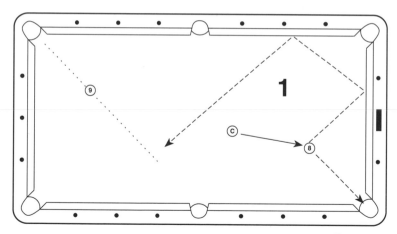

can increase your chances of success almost immediately by following a simple principle: Draw a mental line out from your next object ball and devise a path by which the cue ball will roll *along* that line—not *across* it. This principle is easier to understand when you look at the two diagrams. Diagram 1 shows one option for gaining position on the 9 ball (using low, left English). The problem here is that the cue ball is traveling across the perfect line of aim (dotted line). Unless the ball stops within several inches of that line, the shot is going to be more difficult than it should. In

Diagram 2, the position path has the cue ball traveling along that dotted line *toward* the object ball (this time using high, right English). Now, you can hardly go wrong. Remember, when possible, your chances are always better when the cue ball is traveling along the desired line of aim, not across it.

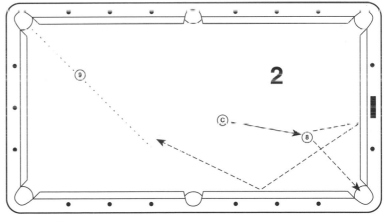

Even with cue ball in hand, players insist on crossing the line.

I can't stress enough the importance of reducing your margin for error on position shots. I've explained the concept of following the line of aim. And I've also suggested a drill for playing the last two balls in a rack. Now, how about combining the two tips. Here's that

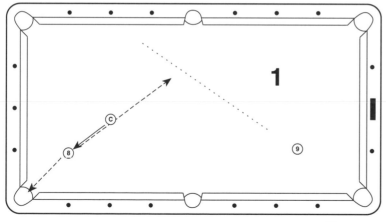

same drill (see Diagram 1), with the 8 ball and 9 ball on the table. With cue ball in hand, the most common choice among beginners—and even some advanced players—is to line up a straight-in shot on the 8 ball. In this case, that means you have to draw the cue ball back for position on the 9 ball. You're confusing principles here.

Sure, you'd like a straight-in shot, but it won't do you any good if you don't get good position for the 9 ball. Again, you've left yourself the task of being too fine. If you don't draw the cue ball enough, or if you draw it too far, your shot on the 9 will be very difficult. It's the "Don't Cross the Line" syndrome. Instead, set up a modest but achievable angle on the 8 and send the cue ball two rails toward the 9 ball. That's "playing the line," and the optimum position for the game-winning 9 ball is anywhere along that line. This eliminates the pitfalls that come with the other option.

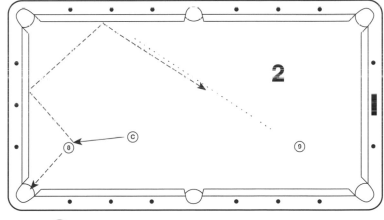

TIP 50—POSITION PLAY

Don't be intimidated by distance when playing position.

Many beginners and intermediates seem to get nervous when their next two shots are at opposite ends of the table. Actually, you'll be surprised when you learn how easily the cue ball travels seven or eight feet. Take the layout in this diagram. The 8 ball and 9 ball

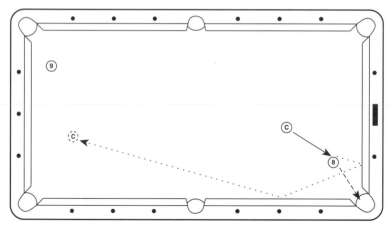

couldn't possibly be much farther away from each other. Yet, this is really a simple shot. You don't need much angle on the 8, so the shot will be easy to make. A little follow is all that's required to get the cue ball up table for position on the 9. Again, don't try to be perfect. Anything above the side pocket will leave you in fine shape.

Avoid temptation. Run like a man.

You're playing 9-Ball and you're faced with two choices: You can run through the entire rack, which is nicely spread around the table, or you can try to shortcut the game by drawing back from the 1 ball for position (a) on a possible 2-9 combination. What would

you do? My choice is easy. I'd shoot the 1 and play position for the 2 ball in the opposite corner (b). Why? Because the 2-9 is not an easy shot, and if you miss, your opponent will likely have an easy run-out. Don't look for shortcuts unless you can't run out. (And even then, look for safeties before wild combinations.)

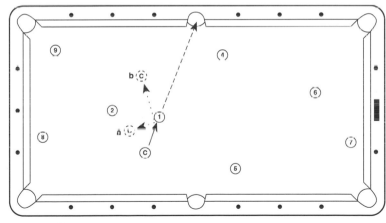

Break the game down into pieces, or you'll go to pieces.

The more developed you become as a player, the further ahead you'll learn to think. Let's go beyond the two-ball drill and incorporate the last four balls of a 9-ball rack. In this case, you don't have cue ball in hand, but you are afforded a nice, easy opening shot on

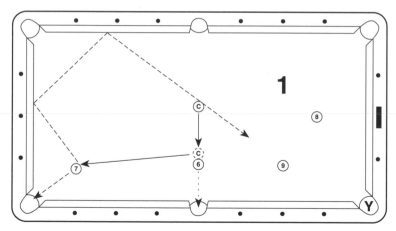

the 6 ball. To the untrained eye, a stop shot on the 6 and angled shot on the 7 would look like the way to begin (Diagram 1). The trouble here is that the key ball on the table is the 8 ball. Again, you have to train yourself to break the game down. If you get proper position on the 8, you've created that two-ball game (8 and 9) you've been practicing. The problem with the path the beginner's chosen is that the cue ball will be travelling from the 7 ball two rails toward the 9 ball. Position on the 9 won't be easy. And, with this path, the cue ball may roll in behind the 9, leaving no shot at the 8, which she or he

will have to pocket in the pocket marked X. The best bet is Diagram 2, in which you use draw on the 6 ball. That allows you to come off the other side rail toward the 8, which you'll shoot into the pocket marked Y. That leaves the 9 out of the picture until you're ready to win the game. Always avoid trouble areas if you can.

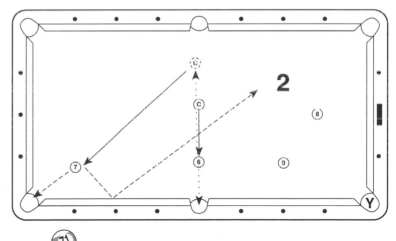

When you don't have an angle, create one.

I've already shown you how straight-in shots can sometimes be detrimental. We've also taken a look at rail-first shots. Here's another example of how you can use several principles to bail you out of a tough situation. Diagram 1 shows the final balls of a 9-Ball game

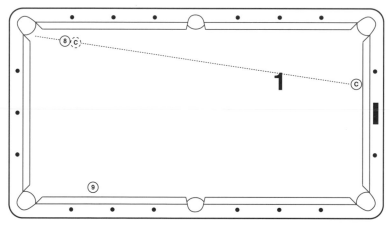

(although it could just as easily be 8-Ball or any other game). As luck would have it, the cue ball is very close to the rail—which means you're limited to using follow. (The rail is more than a half-ball in height.) And because the shot is straight in, you're likely to scratch into the same pocket. Making matters worse, even if you could stop the cue ball dead in its tracks, you'd be in no position to shoot the 9 ball. Diagram 2 shows your only alternative—which is to go rail-first to make the 8 ball and gain position on the 9 ball. The key to executing this shot is to determine where you must strike the rail

to get the cue ball into the same position it would be (dotted cue ball) to pocket the 8 in Diagram 1. Obviously, this is not an easy shot, because maintaining an accurate line when shooting at a cue ball that's frozen to the rail takes a lot of practice. Still, it's your only option in this case.

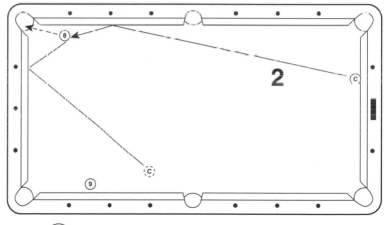

CHAPTER TEN

Eight-Ball Strategy

TIP 54—EIGHT-BALL

The key to the 8-Ball break is to avoid the head ball.

While the straight-on break shot in 8-Ball is the safest route to travel, it is by no means the most effective. As with 9-Ball, the motive on the 8-Ball break is to pocket as many balls as possible, and the best way to accomplish that is to get maximum action from the

balls. Most top players break with the cue ball several inches off the side rail. Aim for the second ball in the triangle. That gets balls moving to the opposite side rail and back, causing a lot of collisions. To avoid scratching, use plenty of draw on the cue ball. That will cause it to swing back toward the side rail.

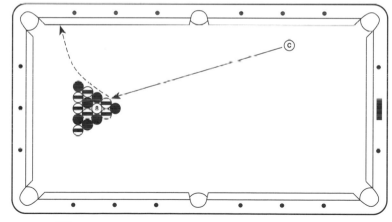

TIP 55—EIGHT-BALL

You won't win in 8-Ball unless you can finish what you start.

Eight-Ball is more of a chess game than most other pocket billiard games. You have a group of balls, as does your opponent. Manuevering around the table requires a plan. Remember, in 8-Ball, the final ball in your grouping is the key ball. And unless you can

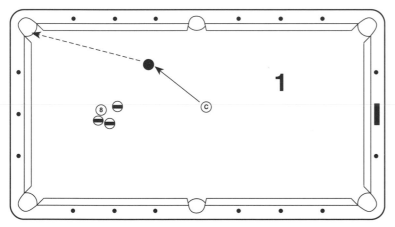

gain position for the 8 ball, don't make the mistake of pocketing the last ball in your group. The more balls you pocket, the easier it is for your opponent to run his balls. If you pocket your last ball but have no shot at the 8, you've played right into your opponent's hands. The layout in Diagram 1 shows your position as you approach the final solid. Being the excellent shooter you are, pocketing the final solid is no problem. But then what? You'd have no real shot at the 8, and dislodging it from that midtable cluster would do more harm than good. Diagram 2 shows the proper approach to this dilemma. Playing safe here serves several purposes. First, it positions the final solid near a pocket—leaving you an easy shot, while closing off that pocket to your opponent. Also, it forces your opponent to negotiate the cluster. Barring a miracle, you should get back to the table with a good chance of polishing off the game.

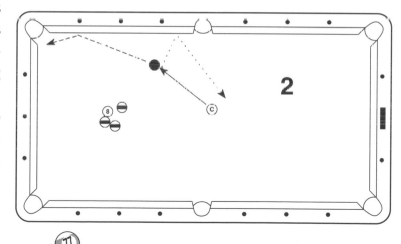

TIP 56—EIGHT-BALL

Pitfalls and plusses when choosing sides in 8-Ball.

How many times have you been playing 8-Ball and your opponent fails to make a ball on the break? You have an overwhelming tendency to run up to the table and sink the ball that's hanging in the jaws of a pocket, right? Well, the key to 8-Ball is running all the

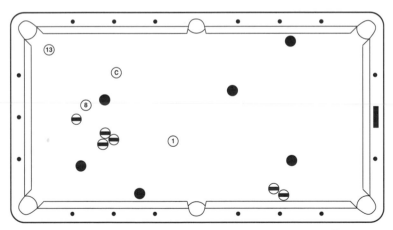

balls in your group. Pocketing one ball doesn't do much if the other balls are unreachable. The layout in the diagram shows a stripe (the 13 ball) sitting at the edge of the corner pocket. But a closer look will show that there are two clusters of striped balls that are going to make a full clearance of the table pretty unlikely. Meanwhile, the solids are nicely spaced around the table. While no shot is quite as easy as the 13 ball, the 1 ball (a solid) offers you the best chance of running multiple balls. Take a shot at the 1, and leave the stripes to your opponent.

Not only will the clusters of striped balls be difficult to break up, but the three-ball cluster near the bottom of the table is awfully close to the 8 ball. It's always a good practice to avoid bumping the 8—it has a sneaky habit of prematurely finding its way into pockets!

The 1 ball, on the other hand, may be slightly more difficult, but if you make it you will gain position on the balls at the upper end of the table. After picking off those balls, you can make your way back down table for the other three solids and the game-winning 8 ball.

TIP 57—EIGHT-BALL

Pool is one of the few games that allows you to cheat!

The key to position play in pocket billiards is control of the cue ball. It's almost always good to have a slight angle on every shot so that you can move the cue ball around the table. Every so often, you'll hear a pro groaning that he "got straight." That means he

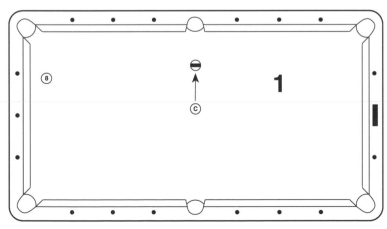

wound up straight-in on his next shot. With no angle, he can't do anything with the cue ball except stop, follow the shot, or draw the cue ball with reverse spin. In Diagram 1, the shooter left himself with no angle to get from the last solid to the 8 ball. He's fearful of draw, because he may draw the cue ball directly back into the side pocket. Following would also be disastrous, and stopping the cue ball won't leave much of a shot at the 8 ball. The trick here is to remember that the pocket is roughly the width of *two* object balls. You don't have to shoot the striped ball directly into the heart of the pocket. By aiming to one side of the pocket, you've created just enough natural angle to follow the cue ball to the side rail and back out for decent position on the 8 ball. For this shot, usc follow and left English. Just like that, from a straight-in shot, you've created an opportunity to get position on the 8 and win the game.

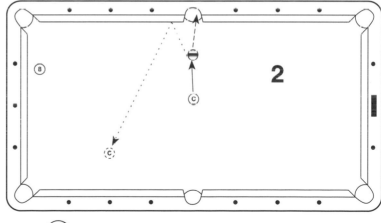

TIP 58—EIGHT-BALL

Winning games means breaking up that old gang of yours.

While it's best to avoid clusters in 8-Ball, you're sometimes stuck with one (or more). The key is to not wait too long before separating the stragglers. In the diagram, there are two stripes to choose from for your first shot, the 11 and the 13 balls. The correct choice

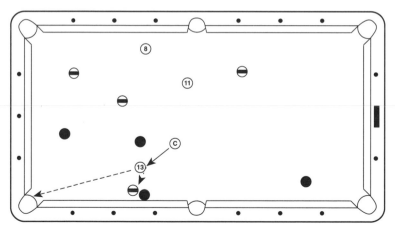

is the 13 ball because it allows you to immediately address the cluster along the rail. By freeing up your problem balls early in the rack, you still have plenty to choose from for your next shot. (The risk in bumping balls is that you lose some control over where the cue ball will end up.)

CHAPTER ELEVEN

Nine-Ball Strategy

TIP 59—NINE-BALL

If you look hard enough, you're bound to catch a break.

Ask any professional player to single out the most important aspect of 9-Ball and, without exception, he or she will tell you it's the break shot. Gaining and maintaining control of the table is absolutely crucial, so the key is to make a ball on the break and control the

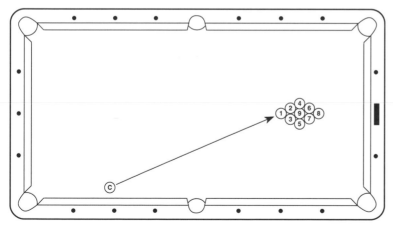

cue ball. I've always found that breaking from the side (as opposed to the middle) of the table produces the most action from the object balls and the most consistent results. Speed is also important. Sometimes it's helpful to take a little speed off the cue ball to maintain control. Remember, the cardinal rule is *don't scratch!*

TIP 60—NINE-BALL

A well-timed bump can add to your run.

Pocket billiards is a mentally challenging game. There are so many options available on every shot, and there is so much to see on the table. Even a simple thing like the shot diagrammed here goes unnoticed more than you can imagine. But top players never miss an opportunity to better their chances. They're always aware. The 6 ball is an easy shot into the side pocket, but the 7 down the rail may not be your favorite type of shot. And you may worry about scratching. Well, there's no rule that says you can't carom the 6 into the side off of the 7, gently nudging the 7 ball into a more comfortable spot.

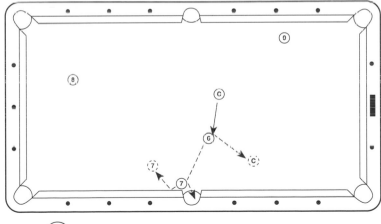

Unless you can run out, better safe than sorry.

In no game can you gain such an immediate and significant advantage with safety play as you can in 9-Ball. By the rules we use on the Pro Tour, failure to make legal contact with the lowest-numbered ball results in ball-in-hand—which means the incoming player can

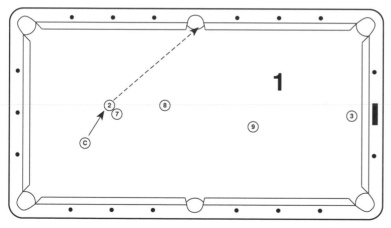

place the cue ball *anywhere* he or she chooses on the table. That's a huge advantage! Once again, the key to gaining this edge comes with recognition. Let's say you approach the table with the layout shown in Diagram 1. It's conceivable that you can pocket the 2 ball in the side pocket. But two things make that an unwise choice. First, cutting a ball into the side pocket is no easy shot. Second, look where the 3 ball is. You're not going to have an easy time getting position for the next shot. Your best friend on the table is the 7 ball. A simple stop shot (see Diagram 2) will send the 2 ball up table and will leave the cue ball safely tucked behind the 7. Your opponent will have to take a stab at the 2. If he or she misses, you'll get cue ball in hand with the object balls nicely spaced around the table. It's an easy way to gain control of the game, and it stems solely from your ability to recognize a good situation when it presents itself.

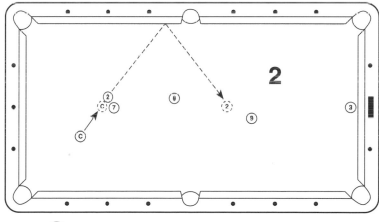

Decision time. Shoot? Or play safe?

There is one constant with pool players of every skill level. No one likes to give up the table. We all want to keep shooting, especially when we're faced with a shot we know we can make. But you have to learn to look beyond the obvious. Take the situation shown in

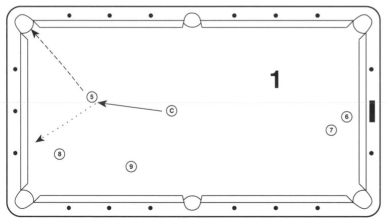

these two diagrams. Diagram 1 shows your initial thought process. You know you can fire the 5 ball right into the corner pocket. But where's the 6 ball? More important, do you have any real chance of getting a good shot at the 6? Not only is it tucked behind a ball at the head of the table, but the 8 ball will probably prevent your cue ball from getting up table (dotted line). No matter how frustrating it is, your best option here is to eschew pocketing the 5 ball in favor of a safety. The benefits of the safety here, albeit not a very glamorous shot, are obvious. By banking the 5 ball up table (dashed line)

and tucking the cue ball in behind the 8 and 9 balls (dotted line), your time away from the table figures to be pretty brief. Now, if your opponent fails to make legal contact with the 5 ball, you'll be back at the table with cue ball in hand. Then you can show off your amazing pocketing abilities. Remember, winning the game is the key.

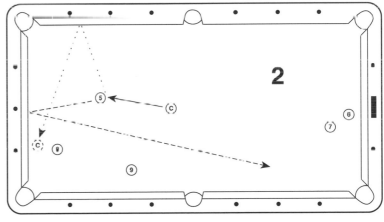

TIP 63—NINE-BALL

As in life, in 9-Ball some risks are worth taking.

In 9-Ball, you're taught never to take a risky combination shot at the 9 ball, because, in doing so, you often risk selling out the game. That's not to say, however, that rule is set in stone. Take the instance here. The 3-9 combination is a low-percentage shot. But what are your options? Most times, you'd shoot the 3 straight in and work toward the 4. A quick survey of the table, however, will tell you that you're going to have a difficult time negotiating a conventional run-out. In this case, there is little risk of selling out, so bypass the straight 3, and go for the combination and the win.

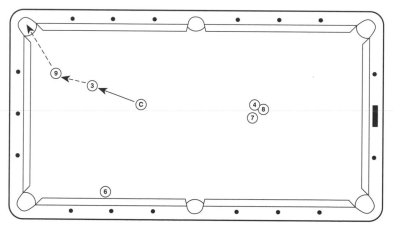

CHAPTER TWELVE

Mental Preparation

TIP 64—PREPARATION

One of the best ways to learn doesn't even involve playing.

There are a lot of ways to become a good pool player. There are numerous instructional books, and there are good, qualified teachers all over the country. You can practice for days in your home or at the local billiard club. But perhaps the best way to learn about the game—and this is exactly how I learned—is to study people who play it well. I used to go to professional tournaments all the time and sit in the bleachers for hours on end watching the best players compete. Talk about an education! I watched what the players did and tried to analyze why. I watched how they changed their bridge from shot to shot, how they studied the table. I learned an amazing amount just studying their characteristics. I'd try to think along with them, then try to figure why they chose a different shot or different pattern. Today, there are videotapes available from tournaments during which matches were taped, with commentary and analysis from some of the top pros. That's a terrific way to learn. Don't just physically learn to play pool. Become a student of the game as well. It'll pay handsome dividends.

TIP 65—PREPARATION

Before you take out your cue, make sure it's properly dressed.

You can know everything there is about pocket billiards, but you'll still miss a key shot if your equipment isn't properly cared for. Pool players are lucky. The only piece of equipment they need is a cue stick. Don't, however, take the cue for granted. There are some very simple but very important tips to caring for your cue. Follow them and you'll never have the cue to blame for your misses! First, the shaft of your cue should be cleaned occasionally. Over time, the shaft picks up powder and dirt, and small burrs sometimes develop. There are cleaning papers and solvents that can clean the cue. Some players still use sandpaper—but it *must* be the finest grade paper you can find. Don't use anything more coarse than 600 grit, or your shaft will begin to look like a sharpened pencil! Also, make sure your tip is rounded, shaped like a nickel. Then, use a rasp or coarser grade sandpaper to scuff the tip up a bit. This is necessary because the tip is leather, and creating small pores will allow the tip to hold chalk. The chalk, of course, is what allows the tip to grab onto the cue ball and impart spin.

TIP 66—PREPARATION

The temptation at the start is to practice 24 hours a day. Don't!

As with other newly discovered sports or hobbies, people tend to jump into pocket billiards with both feet. That's great, but you're best off learning gradually. Too much practice can burn you out or get you frustrated. Even top players have to slow down from time to time. Also, when you do practice, practice against another player. To learn more about the game and gain the proper competitive edge, you should be playing an opponent. Naturally, there are times you won't be able to find an opponent, or you'll want to practice alone. That's fine, too. Just don't get into the habit of practicing alone all of the time. It actually can be counterproductive. Competition keeps you focused. This is particularly true if you're an intermediate or advanced player. Beginners should spend a little more time practicing alone because their game is still in the developmental stages and there are usually plenty of areas for improvement.

CHAPTER THIRTEEN

Tricks of the Trade

A few tricks of the trade make playing even more fun!

All work and no play would have made Steve a dull boy! Trick shots are a lot of fun, and practicing a few will add a little levity to your strenuous practice regimen. Besides, these are not gimmick shots. You can learn plenty about the reactions of balls that are frozen

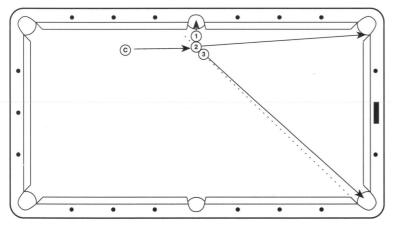

together. The setup of this shot is easy. Place the 1 ball an inch or so out from the side pocket. Freeze the 2 to the 1, aimed directly across to the other side pocket. Freeze the 3 to the 2, aimed at the right tip of the corner pocket (dotted line). Simply strike the 2 ball full. (If the 3 misses, slightly adjust the line of the 2-3.)

TIP 68—TRICK SHOTS

One of the most recognizable trick shots is also one of the easiest.

Virtually every time you see a pro player on a TV talk show, he or she will set up a shot that looks impossible, but even the talk show host can make! Nine out of ten times that shot will be the shot shown here. The setup is a little tricky. Once completed, however, all

you have to do is aim the cue ball through the center. Place the 1 and 2 balls slightly less than a ball's width apart. The 3 and 4 (which should be even with the rail diamonds) should be lined up with the inner edge of the corner pocket (dotted lines). The 5 and 6 should be aimed an inch or so short of the corner pockets (dotted lines).

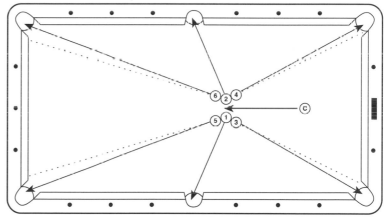

TIP 69—TRICK SHOTS

Once around the table and home.

This tricky little shot has launched a thousand variations, including the shot I used in my first Lite Beer commercial. Place the 3 ball at the edge of the corner pocket. Freeze the 1 ball to the side rail, just below the side pocket. Freeze the 2 ball to the 1, aimed directly

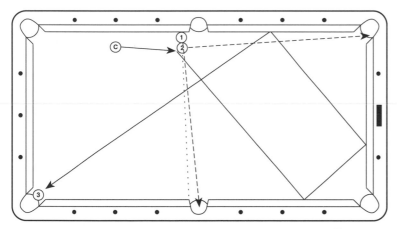

across to the opposite side pocket (dotted line). Place the cue ball about a ball's width from the side rail, even with the second diamond below the side pocket. Strike the cue ball above center and with left English. Aim to hit half (or less) of the 2 ball. The left English will carry the cue ball around the table. Cheers!

TIP 70—TRICK SHOTS

Try to guess which ball goes in first.

Here's another shot that's easy to set up, easy to shoot, but impressive nonetheless. It's a speed shot. (If one ball goes in before the others, you're doing something wrong!) Place the 2 ball in the jaws of the corner pocket. The cue ball should be an inch or so out from the side pocket. Freeze the 1 ball to the cue ball, lined up with the upper left corner pocket. Freeze the 3 ball to the cue ball, aimed directly across to the other side pocket. Aim the cue ball at the lower tip of the corner pocket (dotted line). (The 1 ball, cue ball and 3 ball should form a perfect right angle.) Now just fire at the 2.

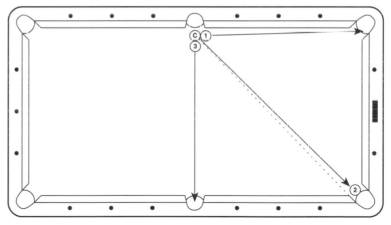

TIP 71—TRICK SHOTS

Show off with your knowledge about kisses.

Like I said, these trick shots aren't gimmick shots. They utilize the same tips and principles that you put to practical use in games. This shot allows you to show off your knowledge about kiss shots. Place the 1 ball on the head spot. Freeze the 2 ball to the 1 so that the 1 is a dead kiss to one corner (remember the perpendicular line between two frozen balls?), while the 2 is a dead combination to the other corner. Knowing that any hit on the top side of the 1 ball will send both the 1 and 2 into the corner pockets, adjust the angle for the cue ball until it consistently goes three rails to sink the 3 ball.

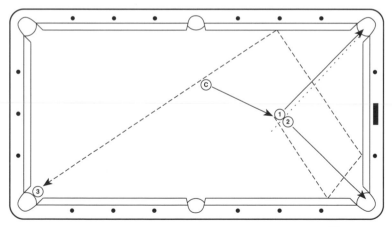

ABOUT THE AUTHOR

From schoolteacher to world champion.

For more than 20 years, Steve Mizerak has been one of the most successful and recognizable pocket billiard players in the world. He is the holder of four Billiard Congress of America U.S. Open titles and two Professional Pool Players Association World Championship crowns, and was inducted into the BCA Hall of Fame in 1980. The Perth Amboy, New Jersey, native was introduced to the game at the tender age of four by his father, a professional baseball player and frequent patron of Madison Recreation—the city's 25-table poolroom. At his father's side, Steve saw the likes of pocket billiard legends Willie Mosconi, Jimmy Caras, and Irving

Crane display their skills at Madison Rec. The youngster was hooked.

A naturally gifted player, Steve excelled at an early age, running more than 50 consecutive balls by 11, and winning the city championship at 13. Although Steve continued to play in city and state tournaments throughout his teens, he opted for college and an education degree. From 1968 to 1981, Steve taught seventh-grade history at William McGinnis Junior High School in Perth Amboy. Despite his busy schedule, Steve continued to play pool—and play it at a higher level than virtually any player in America. From 1970 to 1974, Steve won four consecutive BCA U.S. Open championships, which was considered the most prestigious title in pocket billiards. In 1979, Steve's life was forever changed when he appeared as the star of one of Miller Brewing Company's most entertaining Lite Beer commercials. The sixty-second spot launched Steve's career as one of the game's leading spokespersons and personalities. Despite conducting hundreds of exhibitions each year, Steve managed to keep his game at its competitive best, winning back-to-back world straight-pool titles in 1982 and 1983.

Steve continues to rank among the top professional pocket billiard players in the